U1069948

中国天然气发展报告

（2018）

国家能源局石油天然气司

国务院发展研究中心资源与环境政策研究所

国土资源部油气资源战略研究中心

石油工业出版社

图书在版编目（CIP）数据

中国天然气发展报告. 2018 / 国家能源局石油天然气司，国务院发展研究中心资源与环境政策研究所，国土资源部油气资源战略研究中心编. —北京：石油工业出版社，2018. 8

ISBN 978-7-5183-2828-4

Ⅰ. ①中… Ⅱ. ①国… ②国… ③国… Ⅲ. ①天然气工业-研究报告-中国-2018 Ⅳ. ①F426. 22

中国版本图书馆CIP数据核字（2018）第195346号

出版发行：石油工业出版社
（北京市朝阳区安华里二区 1 号楼 100011）
网　　址：http://www.petropub.com
编 辑 部：(010) 64523766　图书营销中心：(010) 64523633
经　　销：全国新华书店
印　　刷：北京中石油彩色印刷有限责任公司

2018年8月第1版　2018年8月第1次印刷
787 × 1092 毫米　开本：1/16　印张：5.5
字数：130千字

定　价：50.00元
（如发现印装质量问题，我社图书营销中心负责调换）
版权所有，翻印必究

《中国天然气发展报告（2018）》编委会

（以下按姓氏笔画排序）

主　　任：

王一鸣　李凡荣　凌月明

副 主 任：

刘德顺　高世楫　谢承祥

委　　员：

王　晶　王国力　王　婕　史云清

成　赤　刘　冰　李英华　李继峰

张　涛　宋　岩　吴裕根　金淑萍

郭焦锋　韩景宽　鲁尚荣　潘继平

顾　　问：

马永生　王香增　宋永华　李孝堂

金之钧　张玉清　赵文智　贺克斌

郝　芳　贾承造　高德利　康玉柱

黄维和　韩英铎　童晓光　曾兴球

总协调人：

郭焦锋

编写单位：

国家能源局石油天然气司

国务院发展研究中心资源与环境政策研究所

国土资源部油气资源战略研究中心

支持单位：

中国地质调查局发展研究中心

上海国际能源交易中心

清华大学环境学院

中国石油大学（北京）非常规天然气研究院

中国石油规划总院

中国石化石油勘探开发研究院

中海石油气电集团有限责任公司

陕西延长石油（集团）有限责任公司

出版和翻译单位：

石油工业出版社

前　言

世界天然气发展面临的环境形势正发生深刻变化，推进天然气发展的积极因素超过以往任何时期。国际石油价格逐步回归合理区间，美国“页岩革命”走向深入，以绿色发展为特征的新一轮能源转型正在各主要经济体加速推进。中国天然气消费快速增长成为世界天然气较快发展的主要驱动因素。各级政府高度重视，各类市场主体共同发力，产量快速增长，多元供应增强，设施建设加快，销售市场旺盛。在快速发展的同时，中国天然气发展不平衡、不充分的深层次问题和矛盾不断暴露，亟待通过加快发展和深化改革来解决。

天然气是有效治理大气雾霾、推进中国能源生产和消费革命向纵深发展的重要抓手。在决胜全面建成小康社会的关键时期，必须以习近平新时代中国特色社会主义思想为指导，落实党中央、国务院关于深化石油天然气体制改革的决策部署和加快天然气产供储销体系建设的任务要求，着力解决天然气发展不平衡不充分不协调的问题，确保供需基本平衡，民生用气有力保障，市场规律得到充分尊重，天然气产业健康有序可持续发展。

目　录

一、2017年国内外天然气发展状况[1]

世界天然气消费水平和供应能力同步提高，产量增长总体快于消费，延续了近年来天然气供需整体宽松格局。受中韩等国天然气需求大幅上升拉动，世界管道气和液化天然气（LNG）贸易量较快增长，美国LNG出口量大幅增加。受宏观经济稳中向好、能源生产和消费革命持续推进、大气污染防治力度加大等因素的驱动，中国天然气市场呈现供销两旺态势。2017年中国对世界天然气消费增量的贡献达30%以上，成为推动世界天然气发展的主要驱动力。

（一）天然气消费加速增长

亚太市场需求旺盛，世界天然气消费增速稳步提高。 2017年世界天然气消费量达3.67万亿立方米，同比增长3.0%，较过去十年的平均增长水平高0.7个百分点。其中，2017年亚太地区天然气消费同比增长6.2%，是2016年增速的两倍以上，占世界天然气消费总量的21.0%，提高0.6个百分点；欧洲天然气消费同比增长5.5%，逆转过去十年负增长（-0.9%）的态势，占世界天然气消费总量的14.5%，提高0.3个百分点；北美地区天然气消费同比下降0.7%，占比25.7%，下降0.9个百分点；独联体地区天然气消费同比增加0.6%，占

[1] 本节国外储量、生产、消费和贸易的数量和增速数据主要来源于《BP世界能源统计》，国内储量数据来源于自然资源部《全国油气矿产储量通报（2017）》。

比 15.7%，下降 0.4 个百分点；中东地区天然气消费同比增加 5.7%，占比 14.6%，增加 0.4 个百分点。2017 年，天然气消费量超过 1000 亿立方米的国家有美国（7395 亿立方米）、俄罗斯（4248 亿立方米）、中国（2386 亿立方米，不含向港、澳供气）、伊朗（2144 亿立方米）、沙特阿拉伯（1114 亿立方米）、日本（1171 亿立方米）和加拿大（1157 亿立方米）。2017 年世界天然气消费增量的 60% 以上来自于中国、加拿大、沙特阿拉伯、伊朗和德国等国。

多重利好因素驱动，中国天然气消费快速增长。2017 年，中国天然气消费快速增长，呈现“淡季不淡、旺季更旺”态势，全年消费量 2386 亿立方米（不含向港、澳供气），同比增长 14.8%，增速较 2016 年提高 7.2 个百分点。天然气在一次能源消费结构中占比 7.3%，同比提高 0.9 个百分点。其中，城镇燃气和天然气发电消费增长明显，消费量分别由 2016 年的 729 亿立方米、366 亿立方米增至 2017 年的 937 亿立方米和 427 亿立方米，占比分别增至 39.3% 和 17.9%；工业燃料消费量为 760 亿立方米，占比 31.8%；化工用气量延续低迷态势，约为 262 亿立方米，占比由 2016 年的 12.2% 降为 11.0%。2017 年用气人口 3.5 亿人，比首次突破 3 亿人的 2016 年多 0.4 亿人。分地区看，2017 年全国天然气消费量及增量主要集中在环渤海、长三角和西南地区，三个地区天然气消费量 1189 亿立方米，占比达 50%。用气量超过 100 亿立方米的省份（直辖市、自治区）有江苏、广东、四川、新疆、北京、山东六省市，河北、河南、浙江、重庆四省市用气量也接近百亿立方米。

（二）天然气供应保障能力增强

世界天然气资源丰富，支撑天然气供应量快速增长。在需求较快增长的拉动下，世界天然气产量增速明显加快。2017 年世界天然气产量 3.68 万亿立方米，同比增长 4%，与 2016 年相比产量增加约 1300 亿立方米、增速提高 3.1 个百分点。其中，亚太地区天然气产量增长约 5%，达 6075 亿立方米，占世界天然气总产量的比例为 16.5%，同比提高 0.2 个百分点；中东地区产量增长约 4.9%，达 6599 亿立方米，占比 17.9%，与去年基本持平；独联体地区产量增长约 6.2%，达 8155 亿立方米，占比 22.2%，增加 0.5 个百分点；北美地区产量增长 1%，达 9515 亿立方米，占比 25.9%，下降 0.7 个百分点。世界天然气产量居前五位的国家分别是美国（7345 亿立方米）、俄罗斯（6356 亿立方米）、伊朗（2239 亿立方米）、加拿大（1763 亿立方米）和卡塔尔（1757 亿立方米）。

世界天然气资源丰富，资源基础雄厚。当前世界天然气资源开发利用程度总体依然较低，具有持续增储上产的坚实基础。截至 2017 年底，世界常规、非常规天然气资源开发利用率分别约为 20% 和 5%，剩余可采储量 193.5 万亿立方米，储采比 52.6 年。近年来，美国二叠盆地、南美洲东部陆架、东非陆架、东地中海、澳洲西北陆架等领域不断取得重大发现。

中国天然气生产与供应能力持续增强[2]。2017 年，国内

---

[2] 本节国内天然气产量数据来源于国家发展改革委运行局和国家统计局，天然气进出口数据来源于国家海关总署。

天然气产量增长超 100 亿立方米，达 1480.3 亿立方米，同比增长 8.2%。其中：常规天然气产量 1338.7 亿立方米，同比增长 8.1%；页岩气产量 92 亿立方米，同比增长 14.3%；煤层气地面抽采量 49.6 亿立方米、利用量 44 亿立方米，同比分别增长 9.2% 和 13.8%。此外，煤制气产量 26.3 亿立方米，同比增长 34.3%。四川盆地、鄂尔多斯盆地、塔里木盆地和海域四大气区的天然气产量总和为 1233 亿立方米，约占全国天然气总产量的 83.6%。其中，鄂尔多斯盆地产量 450 亿立方米（含煤层气产量 11 亿立方米），约占全国天然气总产量的 30.5%，连续九年为全国第一大产气区；四川盆地天然气产量 395 亿立方米（含页岩气 90 亿立方米），约占全国天然气总产量的 26.8%；塔里木盆地天然气产量 370 亿立方米，约占全国天然气总产量的 25.1%。

中国天然气资源丰富，但勘探开发程度依然较低，常规天然气发展仍有较大潜力。同时，随着技术进步和石油天然气体制改革的不断深入，开发低渗透、深层、深水、火山岩等领域大量的品位低、难动用资源的经济性将逐步显现，非常规天然气资源潜力不断释放。在可预见的将来，国内的天然气生产供应能力将持续提高。

2017 年，中国天然气进口快速增长，进口量 946 亿立方米，同比增长 26.9%。其中，进口管道气 420 亿立方米；进口 LNG 526 亿立方米，同比增长 46.3%。

中国天然气储运设施不断完善，供应能力进一步提升。

2017年，陕京四线、中靖联络线等陆续投入运营；广东粤东、江苏启东LNG接收站投产，储气库扩容稳步推进，中俄东线二期、新疆煤制气外输管道潜江—韶关段以及天津南港、深圳迭福、浙江舟山LNG等重大工程加快建设。截至2017年底，全国已建成投产天然气长输管道7.4万千米，干线管网总输气能力达3100亿立方米/年；累计建成投产地下储气库25座，有效工作气量77亿立方米；已投产液化天然气接收站18座，总接收能力5960万吨/年。同时，集中推进一批互联互通重大节点性工程，打通管输瓶颈，特别是广东管网升压反输西二线、天津地区各气源互保互供等互联互通工程的提前谋划设施，为应对2017—2018年采暖季北方地区天然气供应紧张问题发挥了关键作用。

（三）天然气贸易更加活跃

世界天然气贸易稳步增长，贸易格局持续调整。2017年，世界天然气贸易量1.13万亿立方米，同比增长5.9%，增速提高1个百分点，约占世界天然气消费量的30.9%，同比提高0.9个百分点。其中，管道气贸易量7407亿立方米，同比增长3.7%，与2016年增速相比略放缓0.3个百分点；LNG贸易量3934亿立方米，同比增长10.3%，较2016年增速提高3.6个百分点。

国际LNG贸易空前活跃，参与LNG国际贸易的国家明显增多。国际LNG贸易总量同比增加367亿立方米，出口增量主要来自亚太和北美地区，进口增量主要来自亚洲和欧洲。LNG贸易量在世界天然气贸易量中的占比提高1.4个百分点，达 34.7%，创历史新高。2017 年，澳大利亚 LNG 出口量 759 亿立方米，同比上升 28.2%，出口目标国增至 9 个；美国 LNG 出口量大幅提升，达 174 亿立方米，是 2016 年出口量的 4.1 倍，目标市场在各大洲分布广泛，其中 40.9% 出口至亚太地区，15% 出口到欧洲。此外，安哥拉、马来西亚、尼日利亚、文莱等国和巴布亚新几内亚地区新增 LNG 出口量 110 亿立方米。从进口看，亚洲和欧洲依然是 LNG 的主要进口地区，占世界 LNG 进口贸易量的 89%。其中，欧洲 LNG 进口量 657 亿立方米，同比增长 15.7%；亚洲 LNG 进口量 2835 亿立方米，同比增长 12.9%，增速提高 6.1 个百分点。

国际 LNG 贸易灵活性持续增强。近两年低油价给亚洲 LNG 进口商从“溢价”到“议价”的转变提供了机遇。随着澳大利亚、美国 LNG 项目上产，进口来源多元化，亚洲买家已在合同中引入现货价、交易中心价等混合定价方式，议价能力增强。亚洲 LNG 价格进一步与油价脱钩，天然气独立定价能力有所提升。国际 LNG 贸易合同限制性条款减少，合同灵活性增强。近年来，新签 LNG 合同呈现目的地条款逐步被淘汰、中短期合同占比增加、合同量缩小、现货贸易快速发展等新特点。2017 年，国际 LNG 现货贸易量约 950 亿立方米，占世界 LNG 贸易量的 24.1%，比 2016 年增加 6.1 个百分点；新签 LNG 合同中，期限小于 5 年的合同数量翻番，中长期合同平均年限为 6.7 年，与 2016 年的平均年限 11 年相比显著缩短；单个合同平均气量持续下降，低于 2016 年的

90万吨/年水平。

国际天然气价格有所回升。2017年，欧洲、东北亚进口LNG均价随油价走势呈现不同程度上涨，美国气价也出现上涨。2017年上半年，国际LNG供应相对宽松，东北亚夏季现货价格在5.5美元/MMBtu[3]左右；下半年，特别是进入冬季，受中国“煤改气”、韩国弃核弃煤等能源政策影响，LNG需求超出预期，同时巴基斯坦等新兴市场天然气需求增长较快，国际天然气市场出现时段性供需紧平衡，加上国际油价上涨，导致天然气价格整体上涨。其中，东北亚冬季LNG现货价格一度突破11美元/MMBtu。2017年，美国亨利中心（Henry Hub）均价2.96美元/MMBtu，同比上涨约20.3%；欧洲国家平衡点（NBP）均价5.8美元/MMBtu，同比上涨24.7%；亚洲LNG进口均价7.7美元/MMBtu，同比上涨15.6%。随着国际LNG贸易的快速发展，欧洲、亚太、北美三大市场的天然气价差进一步缩小，亚洲LNG现货与欧洲NBP价格走势趋同。

国内外权威机构预测，未来2～3年，随着澳大利亚、美国、俄罗斯、东非等新建LNG项目陆续上产，到2020年新增LNG产能将达9270万吨并有望突破一亿吨。中长期看，世界天然气市场将延续总体供大于求的态势，供需基本面不支持国际天然气价格持续上涨。

中国天然气进口大幅攀升，进口来源进一步多元化。2017年，中国天然气进口量946亿立方米。其中，管道气进

[3] MMBtu：百万英热单位。

口同比增长 8.8%，约 85% 进口量来自土库曼斯坦，乌兹别克斯坦、缅甸管道气进口量均有所下降。2017 年 10 月，中国石油与哈萨克斯坦石油天然气公司签订了一年期 50 亿立方米的管道气供应合同。2017 年中国 LNG 进口量快速攀升，进口来源目标国进一步多元化。全年进口 LNG 526 亿立方米，进口资源目标国达 22 个，比 2016 年增加 4 个。澳大利亚依然为中国 LNG 进口最大来源国，全年进口 237 亿立方米，同比增长 44.3%；其次是卡塔尔，向中国供应 103 亿立方米，同比增长 50.4%；再次是马来西亚、印度尼西亚等国。2017 年美国向中国出口 LNG 21 亿立方米，比 2016 年增长 7.5 倍，约占同年美国 LNG 出口量的 11.7%，中国已成为美国第三大 LNG 进口国。与管道气进口相比，LNG 进口具有贸易方式灵活多样、供应较安全等优点，叠加非冬季保供期价格相对较低的利好，成为 2017 年中国保障天然气需求增长的主要来源。

2017 年中国天然气进口贸易依然以中国石油、中国石化、中海油三大石油公司为主导，其他企业的天然气进口贸易规模不断扩大。北京燃气、广东九丰、新疆广汇等公司的天然气进口量总和达 20 亿立方米左右，在 2017 年冬季保供方面发挥了积极作用。

（四）中国天然气改革持续发力

2017 年 5 月，中共中央、国务院发布《关于深化石油天然气体制改革的若干意见》。政府有关部门、企业等认真学习领会，扎实推进各项改革任务，相继出台了一系列改革举措。

2017 年，国家发展改革委相继出台《关于加强配气价格监管的指导意见》（发改价格〔2017〕1171 号）、《关于进一步加强垄断行业价格监管的意见》（发改价格规〔2017〕1554 号）、《关于降低非居民用天然气基准门站价格的通知》（发改价格规〔2017〕1582 号）、《关于全面深化价格机制改革的意见》（发改价格〔2017〕1941 号）等文件，进一步加强天然气配送环节价格监管，强化成本监审，明确“准许成本 + 合理收益”的配气定价原则，规定准许收益率不得超过 7%；降低非居民用气基准门站价格，深化非居民用气价格市场化改革，适时放开气源价格和销售价格，完善居民用气价格形成机制，推进居民用气价格逐步与非居民用气价格并轨。上海、重庆天然气交易中心工作有序推进。

为有序推进北方地区冬季清洁取暖，国家发展改革委等多部委联合发布《北方地区冬季清洁取暖规划（2017—2021 年）》（发改能源〔2017〕2100 号），明确要求清洁取暖要坚持“宜气则气、宜电则电”的原则，多种方式并举；进一步强调，“煤改气”要在落实气源的情况下按规划有序推进，并配套了气源保障方案。国家发展改革委、国家能源局发布《关于全面开展天然气储气调峰设施建设运营情况自查和整改的通知》（发改办运行〔2017〕1628 号）等，摸底调查全国储气调峰情况，进一步加强储气调峰能力建设。

为维护油气资源国家所有者权益，调整油气矿业权出让收益比例，促进油气勘查开采，国务院、财政部和自然资源部等部门分别出台《矿产资源权益金制度改革方案》（国发〔2017〕29号）、《矿业权出让收益征收管理暂行办法》（财综〔2017〕35号）等文件，明确规定，除特殊情形外，矿业权一律以招标、拍卖、挂牌等竞争方式出让，能源资源勘查的矿业权出让收益中央与地方分享比例由6：4调整为4：6。财政部、国家税务总局发布《资源税法（征求意见稿）》，对深水油气资源税减征30%，对低丰度、低品位油气资源税减征20%；专门出台政策对页岩气资源税减征30%。同时，持续推进油气勘查开采体制改革，加强油气探矿权竞争性出让。截至2017年，采取竞争方式累计出让常规油气探矿权20个、煤层气探矿权10个、页岩气探矿权22个，新引入上游市场主体32个。其中，2017年挂牌公开出让新疆5个油气勘查区块探矿权。全面实施油气探矿权信息公示制度和监督检查，加大区块核减退出力度，2013—2017年依法注销及核减油气探矿权面积90.9万平方千米。加大油气基础地质调查工作力度，不断开辟勘查新区新领域。积极支持天然气基础设施建设用地，加快用地审查，保障建设项目依法依规及时用地。

二、中国天然气发展遇到的新问题

不论是推进能源生产和消费革命，构建清洁低碳、安全高效的能源体系，还是贯彻落实北方地区冬季清洁取暖要求，天然气都肩负着新的历史使命。打赢蓝天保卫战和打好污染防治攻坚战，天然气也是重要的实现路径之一。2017 年受天然气存量需求快速增长、“煤改气”迅猛发展、进口气供应不稳定等因素影响，中国局部地区个别时段出现用气紧张状况。经各部门、地方、企业间通力合作，供需紧张期虽“有惊无险”地度过，但天然气在快速发展阶段暴露出的问题亟待解决。

（一）产供储销体系建设不完善、体制改革不到位制约天然气协调稳定发展

从 2004 年始，中国天然气已快速发展十余年，呈现规模大、增速快、季节波动性大等特征。同时，在绿色发展政策支持、大气污染防治形势倒逼下，天然气发展模式已由供应驱动演变为需求拉动。但受产供储销体系待健全、体制改革待深入等因素影响，供应侧与需求侧不确定因素增多，发展不平衡问题日益突出，多元化供应体系和市场有序协同机制亟待完善。

勘探开发投入减少造成天然气增储上产跟不上消费快速增长的步伐。中国常规天然气（含致密气）资源探明率

15%，低于世界平均水平（22.5%）。探明储量中未动用占比超过 44%，即使在当前的技术水平下，剩余的经济可采储量 3.9 万亿立方米，其大部分资源的开发成本相对于中缅管道进口气等仍具有明显的价格优势。但受上游主体少、竞争不充分、考核激励机制不足、支持政策不够等因素影响，叠加国际油价低位徘徊、国内资源勘探开发难度较大等客观原因，企业勘探开发投资能力不足、意愿不强，天然气新建产能不足，产量增长乏力。尽管 2017 年全国油气勘查、开采投资分别为 597.5 亿元和 1629 亿元，同比增长 13.3% 和 22.2%，但还没有恢复到 2015 年的投资水平；2016 年全国天然气产能建设规模较 2014 年下降 50%，导致 2017 年市场需求增速达到 14.8% 的情形下，国内天然气产量增速仅为 8.2%。

管网建设速度放缓、互联互通程度不够限制资源调配和市场保供。2014—2016 年期间，天然气市场需求增速放缓，新建管网投资回报率下降，建设资金削减，年均新增里程仅 0.5 万千米。截至 2017 年底，中国天然气干线管道里程约 7.4 万千米，每万平方千米陆地面积对应的管网里程约 77 千米，仅相当于美国的 15%，而管网负载程度（单位里程的天然气消费量 319 立方米 / 千米）相当于美国的两倍。主干管道之间、主干管道与省级管网之间、沿海 LNG 接收站与主干管道之间互联互通程度较低，区域气源“孤岛”或 LNG 孤站多处存在，具备互联互通功能的枢纽站和双向输气功能的管道较少，管网压力不匹配，富余气源和 LNG 接收站能力不能有效利用。截至 2017 年底，三大石油公司管网之间仅实现三处互联互通[4]，对资源调配和市场保供造成较大制约。此外，管网运输和销售分离的改革细化方案仍未出台，尽管供气企业在企业层面开展了天然气运输和销售业务分离的相关举措，但离改革文件精神要求还有较大差距。部分省网公司还保留“统购统销”的经营方式，制约区域市场化竞争格局的形成。

进口气过快增长，资源均衡性和保障性不足，多元化供应体系亟待完善。中国天然气对外依存度快速攀升，进口气量从2010年的175亿立方米迅速增至2017年的946亿立方米。进口来源地虽已超过 20 个国家和地区，但进口气量主要集中在土库曼斯坦、澳大利亚和卡塔尔，三国供应量占中国进口量的70%以上。天然气进口保障的不确定性增加，土库曼斯坦、乌兹别克斯坦、哈萨克斯坦中亚三国与中国地理上属于同纬度，冬季进口管道气易受寒潮影响发生欠量，造成短期供应紧张；LNG 进口受气象、海况、航道等影响，不可控因素增多，亟待建立天然气进口资源保障机制。

责任不落地约束不强，辅助服务市场机制不健全导致储气能力严重不足。2014 年国家发展改革委即印发了 8 号令，提出了地方政府 3 天、供气企业 10% 的储气能力要求，但政策落地和执行力度存在欠缺。以地下储气库和 LNG 接收站储气为主，陆上节约、规模化 CNG 和 LNG 储气为辅，管网互

[4] 2017年底实现天然气管网3处互联互通，分别为西气东输二线和川气东送管道在湖北武穴压气站、西气东输二线与广东省管网在广州压气站、陕京线与安济线在安平压气站实现互联互通。

联互通为支撑的储气系统建设仍然任重道远。同时，储气调峰能力建设监管落实不到位，上游储气指标完成进度滞后，下游用户更是长期过度依赖上游调峰。同时，由于储气调峰市场机制不健全，储气设施市场价值缺少价格实现途径，建设运营投资成本缺少回收渠道；加之辅助服务市场未建立，企业投资积极性不高。截至2017年底，地下储气库形成有效工作气量77亿立方米，占全国表观消费量的3.2%，远低于12%~15%的世界平均水平。18座LNG接收站储气能力40亿立方米，总储气能力严重不足，难以发挥调节季节需求波动、应对供应风险、平抑市场价格等作用。

（二）政策协同性不足、支持力度不够导致天然气行业发展阶段性失衡

一是跨部门、跨行业间统筹协调不畅，全产业链协同发展体系尚未形成。受考核倒逼影响，各地方目前环保政策叠加环保督查集中发力，“煤改气”工程突击整改、集中推进，2013年至2017年的工作任务大量集中在2017年实施，市场平衡状况难以预判。更应当注意到，除居民“煤改气”用气需求外，工业“煤改气”增加的用气需求更为可观。当前的天然气产业不论是供应量还是基础设施均难以支撑短期需求的爆发式增长。同时，目前环保政策上，一方面消费侧需要快速扩大天然气消费，另一方面供应侧环保政策对天然气增产增供形成硬约束。初步估计，当前按环保和生态保护要求需退出的天然气生产加工处理产能即达到千万吨的规模。

二是价格改革还未充分到位。省级门站价格与替代能源挂钩的定价机制尚未实现动态调整，峰谷气价机制还未充分形成，激励用户参与调峰的经济手段还不够，难以发挥价格平衡供需关系的作用。气价交叉补贴和气价倒挂现象仍然存在，影响冬季民生用气保供。市场交易参与程度不高，天然气交易中心线上交易参与的交易主体较少，交易方式和手段较为单一，还有待进一步摸索形成符合中国国情的天然气市场化交易体系。

三是管道等线性工程选线和工程建设协调难度越来越大。受用地用海、保护区等政策限制，部分基础设施项目难以落地。由于管道建设运营未实行分税制，地方收益较少，且承担了管道安全保护责任，地方积极性普遍不高。综合影响下，管道建设运营、油气管道路由协调难度越来越大，征地遇阻、审批不畅等问题突出，制约项目推进。

四是天然气保供和应急处置机制不健全。由于缺少统一标准和监管，在价格双轨制的情况下，极个别责任方出于经济利益考虑，不能保证民生优先用气。互联互通协调机制和商务模式有待完善，尚未建立日常运行和应急状态下的互联互通协调长效机制。商务合作方式仍是“一事一议”，没有形成程序化、规范化、市场化的合作模式。

五是天然气发展的财税支持政策有待进一步配套。相当规模的致密砂岩气储量勘探开发亟须政策支持。页岩气、煤层气开发经济效益依然较低。关键理论、技术和核心装备研发扶持力度有限，深层、火山岩气藏勘探开发核心技术缺乏，深水油气开发关键技术与装备仍以进口为主；页岩气、煤层气开发工程技术与世界先进水平相比仍有较大差距，深部页岩气、陆相页岩气开发核心技术仍有待突破。天然气勘探开发利用的关键技术研发和先进装备国产化亟须加大政策支持力度。

三、加快天然气产供储销体系建设 支撑行业协调稳定发展

天然气是优质高效、绿色清洁的低碳能源。加快天然气开发利用，促进其协调稳定发展，是中国稳步推进能源生产和消费革命，构建清洁低碳、安全高效能源体系的重要路径。加快天然气开发利用，是实现人民对美好生活向往的有机组成部分，更是打赢蓝天保卫战和打好污染防治攻坚战的必然要求。2017 年国内消费爆发式增长，天然气主体能源地位进一步确立。但 2017—2018 年采暖季局部地区供应紧张，也暴露出当前产供储销体系不健全、产业链体制机制改革步调不一致等突出问题。在决胜全面建成小康社会的关键时期，必须以习近平新时代中国特色社会主义思想为指导，落实党中央、国务院关于深化石油天然气体制改革的决策部署和加快天然气产供储销体系建设的任务要求，着力解决天然气发展不平衡不充分不协调的问题，确保天然气供需基本平衡，民生用气有力保障，市场规律得到充分尊重，天然气产业健康有序可持续发展。

（一）中国天然气行业迎来新时代背景下的快速发展期

中国政府高度重视天然气稳定协调发展。国家发展改革委、国家能源局牵头，会同自然资源部、生态环境部、财政部、

住房城乡建设部、交通运输部等有关部委，努力把天然气产供储销体系建设作为一项重点工作抓好；各部门、地方和企业以人民为中心，将保障天然气稳定供应作为重要的民生工程、政治工程，积极谋划、稳妥推进。各部门通过部际联席会议机制和周例会机制，推进财税政策、项目审批等相关扶持政策的出台，高效协调并采取有力举措，推进保供项目快速落地。

全社会逐渐形成大力发展天然气的共识。一是经过多年发展，天然气低碳高效、安全可靠的特性已经成为广泛共识，其清洁能源的定位深入人心。“十九大”报告提出，中国社会主要矛盾已经转化为人民日益增长的美好生活需要和不平衡不充分的发展之间的矛盾。天然气发展事关国计民生，清洁取暖更寄托了人民对绿水青山的向往，加快天然气开发利用已然成为中国推进能源发展转型的重要组成部分。各级政府的高度关注引发社会与媒体的深入聚焦，纷纷看好天然气产业的未来发展趋势。二是在体制改革、考核倒逼、政策支持等引导下，产业链各环节活力逐步释放，支撑中国天然气快速发展。

国际上具有中国天然气快速发展的市场环境。相对宽松的国际 LNG 市场环境助力中国天然气快速发展。国际 LNG 市场迅猛发展，很大程度上突破了传统管道输气的局限，推动了天然气在世界范围内不同市场间的高效流通。截至 2017 年底，全世界已投产 LNG 项目 34 个，共 102 条生产线，总生产能力 3.55 亿吨 / 年。预计到 2020 年，规划在建 LNG 项目共计 15 个，主要分布在非洲、北美、欧洲和亚太地区，规划产能共计约 9270 万吨 / 年。随着澳大利亚、俄罗斯和美国 LNG 在建液化项目逐步投产，预计到 2020 年世界新增 LNG 供应将超过 1 亿吨 / 年。需求方面，中国（含台湾）、韩国、印度等传统亚洲 LNG 进口大国及欧洲，预计未来几年需求旺盛，巴基斯坦、菲律宾、孟加拉国等新兴市场需求增长较快。总体来看，到 2020 年国际 LNG 市场整体供应相对宽松，但仍将呈现个别地区季节性供应紧张的特点。

（二）构建中国天然气协调稳定发展的产供储销体系

构建天然气协调稳定发展的产供储销体系，主要包括加快国内勘探开发、健全海外多元供应、建立多层次天然气储备体系、加快天然气基础设施建设和管网互联互通、精准预测市场需求和建立预警机制、建立完善的天然气供应分级应急预案、建立健全天然气需求侧管理和调峰机制、建立天然气发展综合协调机制、理顺天然气价格、加快体制改革步伐等。天然气产供储销体系的建立不可能一蹴而就、一劳永逸，这是一项系统工程，机制作用的发挥也是渐进式的，需要各地方、各部门及油气企业间的通力合作。

一是加快形成勘探开发有序进入、充分竞争的市场机制。严格执行区块退出，全面实行区块竞争性出让。大力推进央地合资合作，留税于当地，互惠互利，共同发展。加快研究制定难动用、边际储量的竞争性出让机制，多措并举盘活储量存量。加强国有油气企业保障能力考核，企业应服务于国家能源战略，适当降低勘探开发活动的经济指标约束，切实增加有效供应。例如，探索按6%左右的内部收益率标准来推进致密气、页岩气、煤层气等非常规天然气投资项目落地实施。同时，针对四川盆地、鄂尔多斯和新疆地区主要上产区，形成增储上产专项行动方案。统筹平衡天然气开发与环境保护的关系，避免出现“消费侧要求扩大天然气消费，供应侧勘探开发活动处处受限”的困境。

二是健全天然气多元化海外供应体系。海陆并进不断优化中国天然气进口结构和布局，加快推进天然气进口国别地区多元化、运输方式多样化、进口通道多元化和合同模式多样化，积极有序推进进口主体多元化。保障进口，坚持进口贸易和海外投资并重。进口贸易方面，长约和现货两手抓，在增加天然气稳定供应的同时充分发挥现货资源的市场化调峰作用。海外投资方面，突出效益发展，支持企业投资海外天然气上游勘探开发，增强进口天然气资源的掌控能力。加强与重点天然气出口国多双边合作，明确国际合作重点项目，加快推进。

三是加强储气能力建设，建立多层次储备体系。建立以地下储气库和沿海LNG接收站储罐为主，重点地区内陆集约、规模化LNG储罐应急为辅，管网互联互通为支撑的多层次储气调峰系统。供气企业到2020年应拥有不低于其年合同销售量10%的储气能力。城镇燃气企业到2020年形成不低于其年用气量5%的储气能力，同时相应地修订《城镇燃气管理条例》《城镇燃气设计规范》等。地方政府到2020年至少形成不低于保障本行政区域3天日均消费量的储气能力。作为临时性过渡措施，储气能力不达标的，要通过签订可中断供气合同等方式落实调峰能力。各省级人民政府负责统筹推进地方政府和城镇燃气企业储气能力建设，储气设施要集约规模化运营，避免“遍地开花”。加强储气能力建设情况的跟踪调度，对推进不力、违法失信等行为实行约谈问责和联合惩戒。

四是完善天然气基础设施建设和互联互通推进机制。加快规划内管道、LNG接收站等项目建设，专项推进管道互联互通。加强基础设施建设各级规划间，以及基础设施建设规划与国土空间、城乡建设、用地用海、林地占用等规划以及生态保护红线的衔接，特别是要保障项目用地用海需求。落实简政放权精神，简化优化前置性要件审批，积极推行并联审批、前置改后置等方式，缩短项目合规建设手续办理和审批周期。短中期以保障京津冀及周边和汾渭平原天然气安全供应为目标，尽快制定环渤海LNG储运体系实施方案。LNG接收站集约布局、规模发展，鼓励多元主体建设，鼓励站址和岸线资源共用共享；优先考虑现有LNG接收站周边和条件较好、前期工作相对成熟的港区进行扩建和新建。加强站线统筹规划，形成覆盖沿海主要消费区域，与国家主干管网互联互通且向内陆进一步辐射的外输管道。中长期加快完善全国性主干管网，形成对接全国天然气主要消费区和生产区，关键节点和关键线路双向输送，进口和国产气充分连通，多气源、跨区域互济调峰、协同保障的管网体系。对天然气基础设施和互联互通重大工程开展专项督察督办。

五是建立天然气发展综合协调机制。强化供用气双方契约精神，推动供用气企业全面签订合同，鼓励签订中长期合同。“煤改气”坚持“以气定改”，在落实气源前提下有规划地推进；突出京津冀及周边等重点区域，保重点的同时循序渐进。建立完善天然气领域信用体系，对相关合同违约及保供不利的地方和企业，根据情形纳入失信名单，对严重违法失信行为实施联合惩戒。将页岩气、煤层气财政补贴政策延续到“十四五”时期，对致密气新井开发利用量给予财政补贴支持。研究对地下储气库建设的垫底气采购支出给予中央财政补贴，对重点地区应急储气设施建设给予中央预算内投资补助支持。在第三方机构评估论证基础上，研究液化天然气接收站项目进口环节增值税返还政策按实际接卸量执行。积极发展沿海、内河小型 LNG 船舶运输，推动出台 LNG 罐箱多式联运等方面的相关法规政策、标准规范。

六是建立健全天然气需求侧管理，细化预警、调峰和应急机制。统筹考虑经济发展、城镇化进程、能源结构调整、价格政策等多种因素，精准预测天然气需求，尤其要做好冬季取暖期分结构需求预测。建立天然气供需预警机制，及时对苗头性、倾向性、潜在性的供需问题做出预测预警，健全通报和反馈机制，确保供需衔接。坚持天然气合理、高效利用，新增天然气量优先用于城镇居民和大气污染严重地区的生活和冬季取暖散煤替代，重点支持京津冀及周边地区和汾渭平原，实现“增气减煤”。研究出台调峰用户管理办法，建立健全分级调峰用户制度，按照“确保安全、提前告知、充分沟通、稳妥推进”的原则适时启动实施。各地方人民政府要切实承担起民生用气的保供主体责任，县级以上人民政府、上游供气企业和城镇燃气企业要严格按照“压非保民”原则做好分级保供预案和用户调峰方案。建立天然气保供成本合理分摊机制，相应应急支出由保供不力的相关责任方全额承担，参与保供的第三方企业可获得合理收益。

七是理顺天然气价格机制。落实好居民和非居民门站价格水平并轨政策，合理疏导居民用气销售价格。鼓励城镇燃气企业建立上下游气价联动机制，鼓励有条件的地区先行放开大型用户终端销售价格。鼓励和支持供气企业和天然气用户协商建立调峰价格机制。减少供气层级，加强配气环节监管，切实降低过高的省内管道运输价格和配气价格。鼓励用户自主选择资源方和供气路径、形式，大力发展区域及用户双气源、多气源供应。落实地方主体责任，对低收入群体、北方地区农村“煤改气”居民家庭等给予补贴，确保低收入群体生活水平不因价格改革而降低。加强天然气价格监督检查，查处价格违法行为。中央财政要充分利用大气污染防治等资金渠道加大支持力度，保障改革措施平稳实施。有序推进天然气现货市场建设，建成由期货交易平台和若干个区域现货交易平台组成的，覆盖环渤海、华南、华中、川渝等天然气主力消费区，统一开放、竞争有序的天然气市场体系。复制原油期货的成功经验，依托环渤海 LNG 储运体系建设，先行先试探索推出天然气期货。

八是加快天然气体制改革步伐。贯彻落实中共中央国务院《关于深化石油天然气体制改革的若干意见》，推动改革任务落地见效。深化油气勘查开采管理，切实加强国内资源勘探开发力度，尽快出台天然气管网体制改革方案，明确市场预期，鼓励企业投资管网建设。督促企业落实天然气管网等基础设施向第三方市场主体公平开放。加快放开储气地质构造的使用权，配套完善油气、盐业等矿业权的租赁、转让、废弃核销机制以及已开发油气田、盐矿的作价评估机制。鼓励油气、盐业企业利用枯竭油气藏、盐腔（含老腔及新建）与其他主体合作建设地下储气库。

结束语

在应对气候变化、推进能源绿色低碳转型的国际大背景下，遵循“十九大”提出的新两步走战略，大力推进生态文明建设，打赢蓝天保卫战，建设美丽中国，天然气发展迎来了难得的历史机遇。

2018 年，中国天然气仍会是快速发展的一年，预计表观消费量在 2710 亿立方米左右（不含向港、澳供气），同比增长 13.5%，增速较 2017 年有所下降。其中，工业燃料用气将明显增长，消费量约 900 亿立方米，同比增速 18.4%，占比升至 33.2%；城镇燃气和天然气发电依然保持较快增长，消费量分别约为 1050 亿立方米和 500 亿立方米，占比分别达 38.7% 和 18.5%；化工用气态势持续低迷，消费量约 260 亿立方米，占比不足 10%。预计 2020 年、2030 年、2050 年天然气在一次能源消费结构中的占比将分别提升到近 10%、14% 和 15% 左右。

2018 年，中国天然气产业既是充满挑战的一年，更是深化改革之年和天然气产供储销体系建设攻坚之年，必须守住中国天然气发展的安全底线，保证天然气安全平稳供应，满足人民日益增长的用气需求。同时，也要认识到短期内强化调峰等基础设施建设、加快增储上产步伐、构建多元化供应体系都面临严峻挑战，必须要攻坚克难，以钉钉子的精神做实做细做好各项工作。

2018 年，《中国天然气发展报告》白皮书已成功推出三年，搭建了一个推进中国能源大转型与探索天然气产业健康、快速发展的交流沟通平台。期待 2018 年《中国天然气发展报告》的发布，能进一步激发社会各界凝聚共识，共同推进天然气产供储销体系建设。在此，我们诚挚地感谢各相关部门、研究机构、行业学会、企业、国际机构以及众多专家的大力支持和帮助。

China Natural Gas Development Report

(2018)

Oil and Gas Department, National Energy Administration

Institute for Resources and Environment Policies, Development Research Center of the State Council

Center for Oil and Gas Resource Strategies, Ministry of Land and Resources

Petroleum Industry Press

China Natural Gas Development Report (2018)

Editorial Board

(Following the surname stroke order)

Chairpersons:

Wang Yiming Li Fanrong Ling Yueming

Deputy Chairpersons:

Liu Deshun Gao Shiji Xie Chengxiang

Committee Members:

Wang Jing Wang Guoli Wang Jie Shi Yunqing

Cheng Chi Liu Bing Li Yinghua Li Jifeng

Zhang Tao Song Yan Wu Yugen Jin Shuping

Guo Jiaofeng Han Jingkuan Lu Shangrong Pan Jiping

Advisors:

Ma Yongsheng Wang Xiangzeng Song Yonghua Li Xiaotang

Jin Zhijun Zhang Yuqing Zhao Wenzhi He Kebin

Hao Fang Jia Chengzao Gao Deli Kang Yuzhu

Huang Weihe Han Yingduo Tong Xiaoguang Zeng Xingqiu

Coordinator:

Guo Jiaofeng

Principal Institutions:

Oil and Gas Department, National Energy Administration

Institute for Resources and Environment Policies, Development Research Center of the State Council

Center for Oil and Gas Resource Strategies, Ministry of Land and Resources

Supported Institutions:

Development and Research Center of China Geological Survey

Shanghai International Energy Exchange Corporation

School of Environment, Tsinghua University

Unconventional Natural Gas Institute (UNGI) of China University Of Petroleum-Beijing (CUPB)

China Petroleum Planning and Engineering Institute (CPPEI)

Sinopec Petroleum Exploration and Production Research Institute

Gas & Power Group of CNOOC

Shaanxi Yanchang Petroleum (Group) Co., Ltd.

Published and translated by:

Petroleum Industry Press

Preface

The environmental situation facing the world's natural gas development is undergoing profound changes, and the positive factors for promoting the development of natural gas are greater than ever before. International oil prices have gradually returned to a reasonable range, the "shale revolution" in the United States has penetrated deeper, and a new round of energy transformation characterized by green development is speeding up in all major economies. The rapid growth of natural gas consumption in China has become the main driving force for the relatively rapid development of natural gas in the world. Governments at all levels attach great importance to natural gas development. With all kinds of market players making joint efforts, they have achieved rapid output growth, diversified supply enhancement, quickened facility construction and an exuberant sales market. While developing rapidly, the deep-seated problems and contradictions of uneven and insufficient development of natural gas in China are constantly exposed, which need to be solved by accelerating development and deepening reform.

Natural gas is a critical action point for effectively controlling atmospheric haze and promoting the development of

China's energy production and consumption revolution in depth and breadth. In the crucial period of securing a decisive victory in building a moderately prosperous society in all respects, we must be guided by Xi Jinping's Thought of Socialism with Chinese Characteristics for a New Era to implement the decisions and arrangements of the CPC Central Committee and the State Council on deepening the reform of the oil and natural gas system, and the tasks and requirements of speeding up the construction of the natural gas production, supply, storage, and marketing system, so as to solve the problem of the unbalanced and uncoordinated development of natural gas. This will ensure that supply and demand will be basically balanced, people's gas consumption will be effectively guaranteed, market rules will be fully respected, and that the natural gas industry will develop healthily, orderly, and sustainably.

CONTENTS

1. Global Natural Gas Development Status in 2017[1]

The world's natural gas consumption level and supply capacity have increased simultaneously, with output growth generally faster than consumption, continuing the overall loosening pattern of natural gas supply and demand in recent years. Stimulated by the sharp increase in natural gas demand in China and South Korea, the world trade in pipeline gas and liquefied natural gas (LNG) has grown rapidly, and US LNG exports have undergone a significant increase. Driven by such factors as the macro economy being stable and moving in a positive direction, continuous advancement of energy production and consumption revolution, and increased prevention and control of atmospheric pollution, China's natural gas market has exhibited a boom in supply and marketing. In 2017, China's contribution to world natural gas consumption increased by over 30%. China became the main driving force for the development of natural gas in the world.

[1] In this section, data on foreign reserves, production, consumption, and trade volume and growth rate are mainly from *BP Statistical Review of World Energy*. Domestic reserves data are from *National Oil and Gas Reserves Bulletin (2017)* published by Ministry of Natural Resources.

(1) Accelerated growth in natural gas consumption

Demand in the Asia-Pacific market was strong, and the growth rate of natural gas consumption in the world indicated a steady increase. In 2017, world natural gas consumption reached 3.67 trillion cubic meters, a year-on-year increase of 3.0%, and 0.7 percentage points higher than the average growth rate of the past decade. Among them, natural gas consumption in the Asia-Pacific region increased by 6.2% year-on-year in 2017, more than double the growth rate in 2016. It accounted for 21.0% of the world's total natural gas consumption and exhibited a 0.6 percentage point increase. European natural gas consumption increased by 5.5% over the same period last year, reversing the negative growth (-0.9%) in the past decade. It accounted for 14.5% of the world's total natural gas consumption and showed a 0.3 percentage point increase. Natural gas consumption in North America fell by 0.7% year-on-year, accounting for 25.7%, down 0.9 percentage points. The consumption in the CIS region increased by 0.6% year-on-year, accounting for 15.7%, down 0.4 percentage points. That in the Middle East increased by 5.7% over the same period last year, accounting for 14.6%, an increase of 0.4 percentage points. In 2017, countries with more than 100 billion cubic meters of natural gas consumption were the United States (739.5

billion cubic meters), Russia (424.8 billion cubic meters), and China (238.6 billion cubic meters, excluding gas supply to Hong Kong and Macao), Iran (214.4 billion cubic meters), Saudi Arabia (111.4 billion cubic meters), Japan (117.1 billion cubic meters) and Canada (115.7 billion cubic meters). More than 60% of the increase in world natural gas consumption in 2017 was contributed by countries including China, Canada, Saudi Arabia, Iran and Germany.

Driven by multiple positive factors, China's natural gas consumption has been growing rapidly. In 2017, China's natural gas consumption grew rapidly, showing a trend of "not weak in the off-season and more prosperous in the peak season." The annual consumption was 238.6 billion cubic meters (excluding gas supply to Hong Kong and Macao), a year-on-year increase of 14.8%. The growth rate was 7.2 percentage points higher than that of 2016. Natural gas accounted for 7.3% of the primary energy consumption structure, up 0.9 percentage points year-on-year. Among them, urban gas and natural gas power generation consumption increased significantly, from 72.9 billion cubic meters and 36.6 billion cubic meters in 2016 to 93.7 billion cubic meters and 42.7 billion cubic meters in 2017 respectively, and the proportion increased to 39.3% and 17.9%, respectively. Industrial fuel consumption was 76 billion cubic meters, accounting for 31.8%. Chemical engineering gas consumption continued to be sluggish, about 26.2 billion cubic meters, accounting for 11.0% from 12.2% in 2016. In 2017, the population consuming gas was 350 million, 40 million more than in 2016 when the population consuming gas made a breakthrough of over 300 million. Divided by region, the national natural gas consumption and increment in 2017 were mainly concentrated in the Bohai Rim, the Yangtze River Delta and the Southwest. Natural gas consumption in the three regions was 118.9 billion cubic meters, accounting for 50%. The provinces (municipalities, autonomous regions) with more than 10 billion cubic meters of gas consumption include Jiangsu, Guangdong, Sichuan, Xinjiang, Beijing, and Shandong. The consumption in Hebei, Henan, Zhejiang, and Chongqing was also close to 10 billion cubic meters.

(2) Enhanced natural gas supply support capacity

The world's natural gas resources are abundant enough to support the rapid growth of natural gas supply. Stimulated by the rapid growth in demand, the world's natural gas production growth rate has significantly accelerated. In 2017, the world's natural gas production was 3.68 trillion cubic meters, a year-on-year increase of 4%. Compared with 2016, the output increased by about 130 billion cubic meters, and the growth rate increased by 3.1 percentage points. Among them, natural gas production in the Asia-Pacific region increased by about 5% to 607.5 billion cubic meters, accounting for 16.5% of the world's total natural gas output, up 0.2 percentage points year-on-year. Production growth in the Middle East was about 4.9%, reaching 659.9 billion cubic meters, accounting for 17.9%, basically the same as last year. The output of the CIS region increased by about 6.2%, reaching 815.5 billion cubic meters, accounting for 22.2%, an increase of 0.5 percentage points. Production increase in North America was 1%, to 951.5 billion cubic meters, accounting for 25.9%, down 0.7 percentage points. The world's top five producers of natural gas are the United States (734.5 billion cubic meters), Russia (635.6 billion cubic meters), Iran (223.9 billion cubic meters), Canada (176.3 billion cubic meters) and Qatar (175.7 billion cubic meters).

The world has a solid foundation for abundant natural gas resources. At present, the degree of development and utilization of natural gas resources in the world is still low, and it has a solid foundation for a continuous increase in reserves and production. By the end of 2017, the utilization rate of conventional and unconventional natural gas resources in the world was about 20% and 5% respectively. The remaining recoverable reserves were 193.5 trillion cubic meters, with a reserve-production ratio of 52.6 years. In recent years, major discoveries have been made in the field including the Permian Basin in the US, the eastern shelf of South America, the East African shelf, the Eastern Mediterranean, and the northwest shelf of Australia.

China's natural gas production and supply capacity continue to increase.[2] In 2017, domestic natural gas production increased by more than 10 billion cubic meters, reaching 148.03 billion cubic meters, an increase of 8.2%. Among them: Conventional natural gas production was 133.87 billion cubic meters, up 8.1% year-on-year; shale gas production was 9.2 billion cubic meters, an increase of 14.3% over the same period last year; surface extraction and utilization of coalbed methane (CBM) was 4.96 billion cubic meters and 4.4 billion cubic meters, respectively, reporting a year-on-year growth of 9.2% and 13.8%. In addition, the output of coal-to-gas production was 2.63 billion cubic meters, a year-on-year increase of 34.3%. The total natural gas production in the four major gas zones, Sichuan Basin, Ordos Basin, Tarim Basin and the sea area was 123.3 billion cubic meters, accounting for 83.6% of China's

[2] The domestic natural gas production data are sourced from the Economic Operation and Regulation Bureau of the National Development and Reform Commission and National Bureau of Statistics. The natural gas import and export data are from the General Administration of Customs.

total natural gas output. Among them, the output of Ordos Basin was 45 billion cubic meters (including 1.1 billion cubic meters of coalbed methane), accounting for about 30.5% of the total natural gas output of the whole country. Ordos Basin has been the largest gas producing area in the country for nine consecutive years. Sichuan Basin produced 39.5 billion cubic meters of natural gas (including 9 billion cubic meters of shale gas), accounting for 26.8% of the country's total natural gas output. Tarim Basin had a production rate of 37 billion cubic meters, accounting for about 25.1% of the total natural gas output.

China has abundant natural gas resources, but a low level of exploration and development. There is still great potential for conventional natural gas development. At the same time, with the advancement of technology and the deepening of the reform of the oil and gas system, the development of low-grade, difficult-to-use resources in the fields of low permeability, deep stratum, deep water and volcanic rocks will gradually show its economic efficiency. The potential of unconventional natural gas resources will be continuously released. Domestic natural gas production and supply capacity will continue to improve in the foreseeable future.

In 2017, China's natural gas imports grew rapidly, with an amount of 94.6 billion cubic meters, a year-on-year increase of

26.9%. Among them, imported pipeline gas was 42 billion cubic meters; imported LNG 52.6 billion cubic meters, an increase of 46.3%.

China's natural gas storage and transportation facilities have been continuously improved, resulting in enhanced supply capacity. In 2017, the Fourth Shaanxi-Beijing Line and the Zhongwei-Jingbian Liaison Line were put into operation one after the other. The LNG receiving stations in the East of Guangdong and Qidong, Jiangsu, were put into production, and the expansion of gas storage depots were advanced steadily. The construction of major projects such as the Second Phase of the Eastern Sino-Russian Line, the Qianjiang-Shaoguan section of the Xinjiang coal-to-gas pipeline, and LNG in Nangang, Tianjin, Diefu, Shenzhen, and Zhoushan, Zhejiang was accelerated. By the end of 2017, 74,000 kilometres of long-distance natural gas pipelines have been completed and put into production, with the total gas transmission capacity of the trunk pipeline network reaching 310 billion cubic meters per year. 25 underground gas storage depots have been built and put into production, with an effective working gas volume of 7.7 billion cubic meters. 18 LNG receiving stations have been put into operation, with a total receiving capacity of 59.6 million tons per year. In the meantime, efforts have been focused on promoting a number of major interconnection node projects to clear bottlenecks in pipeline transportation, in particular the planning for facilities for such interconnection projects as the Second West Line of Pressure Boosting and Reverse Transportation of Guangdong Pipeline Network, and the mutual guarantee of supply among all gas sources in Tianjin. The work has played a key role in coping with the shortage of natural gas supply in the northern region during the heating season 2017—2018.

(3) More dynamic natural gas trade

The world natural gas trade has grown steadily, and the trade pattern has continued to adjust. In 2017, the volume of world natural gas trade was 1.13 trillion cubic meters, an increase of 5.9% over the same period last year, with the growth rate increased by 1 percentage point. The trade volume accounted for 30.9% of the world's natural gas consumption, an increase of 0.9 percentage point over the same period last year. Among them, the pipeline gas trade volume was 740.7 billion cubic meters, a year-on-year increase of 3.7%, a slight slowdown of 0.3 percentage points of growth rate compared with that in 2016. The LNG trade volume was 393.4 billion cubic meters, a year-on-year increase of 10.3%, an increase of 3.6 percentage points of growth rate compared with that in 2016.

The international LNG trade has been more active than ever before, and the number of countries participating in LNG international trade has increased significantly. The total volume of international LNG trade increased by 36.7 billion cubic meters year-on-year. The increase in exports mainly came from the Asia. Pacific and North America, and the increase in imports was mainly from Asia and Europe. The share of LNG trade volume in world natural gas trade increased by 1.4 percentage points to 34.7%, a record high. In 2017, Australia exported 75.9 billion cubic meters of LNG, up 28.2% from a year earlier, with export target countries rising to 9. U.S. LNG exports surged to 17.4 billion cubic meters, 4.1 times the 2016 level. The export target markets were widely spread across continents. Among them, 40.9% of LNG went to the Asia-Pacific region and 15% to Europe. In addition, Angola, Malaysia, Nigeria, Brunei and other countries, and the Papua New Guinea regions have added 11 billion cubic meters of LNG exports. In terms of imports, Asia and Europe remained the main import regions of LNG, accounting for 89% of the world's LNG import trade. Among them, Europe imported 65.7 billion cubic meters of LNG, up 15.7% from a year earlier; Asia imported 283.5 billion cubic meters of LNG, up 12.9% year-on-year, and the growth rate was 6.1 percentage points higher.

International LNG trade flexibility continued to improve. The low oil prices in the past two years have provided an opportunity for Asian LNG importers to shift from "premium" to "bargaining." With the increasing production of LNG in Australia and the United States and the increasingly diversified sources of imports, Asian buyers have enhanced their bargaining power by introducing mixed pricing methods such as the spot price and transaction centre price in the contract. LNG prices in Asia have further decoupled from oil prices and the independent pricing power for natural gas has improved. The restrictive clauses of international LNG trade contracts have been reduced, and contract flexibility has been increased. In recent years, the newly signed LNG contracts have been characterized by the gradual elimination of destination terms, the increase in the proportion of medium and short-term contracts, the shrinking of contract volume, and the rapid development of spot trade. In 2017, international LNG spot trade volume was about 95 billion cubic meters, accounting for 24.1% of the world's LNG trade, an increase of 6.1 percentage points over 2016. Among the newly signed LNG contracts, the number with a duration of fewer than 5 years doubled, and the average length of medium and long-term contracts was 6.7 years, significantly shorter than the average of 11 years in 2016. The average gas volume of a single contract continued to decline, lower than the 2016 level of 900,000 tons per year.

International natural gas prices have rebounded. In 2017, the average price of imported LNG in Europe and Northeast Asia increased with the trend of oil price, and the US gas price also rose. In the first half of 2017, international LNG supply was relatively generous, with spot prices in Northeast Asia standing at about USD 5.50/MMBtu[3] in summer. In the second half, especially in the winter, affected by China's "changing coal into gas" policy and South Korea's nuclear and coal abandonment policy, demand for LNG has exceeded expectations. At the same time, the demand for natural gas in Pakistan and other emerging markets was growing rapidly. As a result, the international natural gas market has experienced a tight balance between supply and demand in a short period of time. In addition, the rise in international oil prices has led to an overall rise in the price of natural gas. In northeast Asia, winter LNG spot prices briefly exceeded USD 11 / MMBtu. In 2017, the average price at the Henry Hub in America was USD 2.96 / MMBtu, up about 20.3% from a year earlier. The average price of national balance point (NBP) in Europe was USD 5.80 / MMBtu, an increase of 24.7% year-on-year. The average LNG import price in Asia was

---

❸ Million British thermal unit.

USD 7.70 / MMBtu, up 15.6% over the same period last year. With the rapid development of international LNG trade, the price difference of natural gas in three major markets of Europe, Asia Pacific and North America further narrowed. Asian LNG spot prices tend to converge with European NBP prices.

Authorities at home and abroad predict that in the next two to three years, with new LNG projects in Australia, the United States, Russia, and East Africa increasing production, newly added LNG capacity will reach 92.70 million tons and is expected to exceed 100 million tons by 2020. In the medium and long term, the world natural gas market will continue the overall situation of oversupply. Supply and demand fundamentals will not support the continued rise in international natural gas prices.

China's natural gas imports have soared, and sources of imports have been further diversified. In 2017, China's natural gas imports were 94.6 billion cubic meters. Among them, the pipeline gas imports increased by 8.8% over the same period last year, about 85% of which came from Turkmenistan. Those from Uzbekistan and Myanmar have declined. In October 2017, China National Petroleum Corporation (CNPC) signed a one-year, 5 billion cubic meter pipeline gas supply contract with Kazakhstan Oil and Gas Company. China's LNG imports rose rapidly, and the import target countries were further diversified in 2017. The annual import of LNG was 52.6 billion cubic meters, with 22 countries targeted for import resources, an increase of 4 from 2016. Australia remained the largest source of China's LNG imports, with annual imports of 23.7 billion cubic meters, up 44.3% from a year earlier. Qatar followed Australia by supplying 10.3 billion cubic meters, up 50.4% year-on-year. Then there were the countries including Malaysia and Indonesia. In 2017, the United States exported 2.1 billion cubic meters of LNG to China, a 7.5-fold increase over 2016, accounting for 11.7% of the U.S. LNG exports in the same year. China has become the third largest LNG importer in the United States. Compared with the import of pipeline gas, LNG imports have the advantage of flexible trade mode and safe supply. Coupled with relatively low prices for the non-winter guarantee period, LNG imports became the main source for satisfying China's gas demand growth in 2017.

China's natural gas import trade was still dominated by CNPC, Sinopec and CNOOC in 2007, while other companies continued to expand their scale of natural gas import trade. Companies such as Beijing Gas, Guangdong Jovo and Xinjiang Guanghui imported about 2 billion cubic meters of natural gas, which played an active role in guaranteeing the supply of natural gas in the winter of 2017.

(4) Continuous efforts to reform China's natural gas industry

In May 2017, the Central Committee of CPC and the State Council issued *Opinions on Deepening the Reform of the Oil and Gas System*. Relevant government departments and enterprises have conscientiously studied and understood the *Opinions*, carried forward various reform tasks in a down-to-earth manner, and issued a series of reform measures successively.

In 2017, the National Development and Reform Commission (NDRC) successively introduced the *Guidance for Strengthening Regulation of Gas Distribution Price* (FGJG No. 1171〔2017〕), *Opinions on Further Strengthening Price Regulation in Monopolized Industries* (FGJGG No. 1554〔2017〕), *Notice on Lowering the Price of Non-Resident Gas Reference Gate Stations* (FGJGG No. 1582〔2017〕), *Opinions on Comprehensively Deepening the Reform of the Pricing Mechanism* (FGJG No.1941〔2017〕), etc. The documents were dedicated to further strengthen price supervision in the natural gas distribution sector, to enhance cost supervision and examination, and to clarify the gas distribution pricing principle of "permitted cost plus reasonable return" by stipulating that the permitted rate of return should not exceed 7%. They were also aimed to lower the price of non-resident gas reference gate stations, to deepen the market-oriented reform of gas prices for non-residents, to liberalize gas supply prices and sales prices in due course, to improve the mechanism for the formation of residential gas prices, and to promote the gradual integration of residential gas prices with those of non-residents. Natural gas trading centres in Shanghai and Chongqing have been advancing their work in an orderly manner.

For the purpose of promoting a clean and warm winter in the northern region in an orderly manner, the National Development and Reform Commission and other ministries and commissions jointly issued the *Winter Clean Heating Plan for the North Region* (2017—2021) (FGNY No. 2100〔2017〕). In the plan, it is clearly required that for clean heating the principle of "use gas or electricity when appropriate" should be adhered to and various methods should be developed simultaneously. It is further emphasized that "changing coal into gas" should be carried forward in an orderly manner according to the plan on the condition that gas sources are guaranteed. Accordingly, a gas source guarantee scheme is provided as a complement to the plan. The National Development and Reform Commission and National Energy Administration issued the *Notice on the Comprehensive Self-examination and Rectification of the Construction and Operation of Natural Gas Storage and Peak Shaving Facilities* (FGBYX No. 1628〔2017〕) etc. It is aimed to make a thorough investigation of the peak-shaving situation of natural gas storage throughout the country and to further strengthen the capacity of gas storage peak shaving.

To safeguard the rights and interests of the State owners of oil and gas resources, adjust the sharing ratio of income from the transfer of oil and gas mining rights, and promote the exploration and exploitation of oil and gas, the State Council, Ministry of Finance, Ministry of Natural Resources, and other departments respectively issued the *Plan for the Reform of the Mineral Resource Royalty System* (GF No. 29〔2017〕), the *Interim Measures for the Administration of the Collection of Income from the Transfer of Mineral Rights* (CZ No. 35〔2017〕) etc. In the documents, it is clearly stipulated that except for special circumstances, all mining rights should be transferred by competitive means such as bidding, auction and listing; the sharing ratio of income from mining rights transfer in energy resources exploration should be adjusted from 6:4 to 4:6 between the central and local governments.The Ministry of Finance and the State Administration of Taxation issued the *Law of the People's Republic of China on Resource Tax (Consultation Paper)* to reduce the tax on deepwater oil and gas resources by 30% and the tax on low-abundance and low-grade oil and gas resources by 20%. In addition, a special policy was introduced to reduce the tax on shale gas resources by 30%. In the meantime, the oil and gas exploration and exploitation system have been further promoted to enhance the competitive transfer of oil and gas exploration rights. By 2017, 20 conventional oil and gas exploration rights, 10 coalbed methane exploration rights and 22 shale gas exploration rights have been transferred by means of competition, with 32 new upstream market entities introduced. Among them, the listed sale of 5 exploration rights of oil and gas exploration blocks in Xinjiang were accomplished. By comprehensively implementing the oil and gas exploration rights information publicity system and the supervision and inspection of the system, and increasing efforts on checking and reducing blocks and their withdrawal, the oil and gas exploration rights that have been cancelled and reduced covered an area of 909,000 square kilometres in 2013—2017. Efforts have been made to intensify the basic geological survey of oil and gas and to open up new areas and fields for exploration. Efforts have also been channelled into actively supporting the use of land for natural gas infrastructure construction, speeding up the review of land use, and ensuring that construction projects use land according to regulations and in a timely manner.

2. New Problems Encountered in the Development of Natural Gas in China

Natural gas is shouldering a new historical mission to promote the revolution of energy production and consumption, to build a clean, low-carbon, safe and efficient energy system, and to implement the requirements of clean heating in winter in northern China. Natural gas is also one of the crucial paths to protect the blue sky and to prevent environmental pollution. In 2017, under the influence of the rapid growth of natural gas storage demand, the rapid development of "changing coal into gas" and the unstable supply of imported gas, gas shortages occurred in individual time periods in parts of China. Thanks to the concerted efforts of various departments, localities and enterprises, China weathered the period of tight supply and demand. However, the problems exposed in the rapid development stage of natural gas need to be solved urgently.

(1) Imperfect production, supply, storage, and marketing systems and inadequate institutional reform have restricted the coordinated and stable development of natural gas.

Since 2004, China's natural gas has been developing

rapidly for more than ten years, showing the characteristics of large-scale, fast growth rate and large seasonal fluctuation. In the meantime, under the support of green development policies and the situation of air pollution prevention, the natural gas development model has evolved from supply-driven to demand-driven. However, due to imperfect production, supply, storage, and marketing systems and inadequate institutional reform, supply-side and demand-side uncertainties increased, and the imbalance in development has become increasingly prominent. Therefore, the diversified supply system and the market coordination mechanism need to be improved.

Due to the decrease in exploration and development investment, the increase in natural gas reserves and production could not keep pace with the rapid growth of consumption. The proven rate of conventional natural gas (including tight gas) in China is 15%, which is lower than the world average (22.5%). Un-utilized reserves account for more than 44% of the proven reserves. Even at the current level of technology, the remaining economically recoverable reserves are 3.9 trillion cubic metres. The development cost of most of such reserves still has obvious price advantage compared with the imported gas from the Sino-Burmese pipeline. However, there are few upstream enterprises, and the competition is not great enough. There are insufficient evaluation and incentive mechanisms and support policies. The international oil prices are hovering around a low level. And it is difficult to explore and develop domestic resources. As a result of these difficulties, the enterprises lack the ability and willingness to invest in exploration and development. As a result, new natural gas production capacity is insufficient, and the output growth is weak. In 2017, China's investment in oil and gas exploration and exploitation was 59.75 billion yuan and 162.9 billion yuan respectively, up 13.3% and 22.2% over the same period last year. However not yet reaching the level of investment in 2015. In 2016, China's natural gas production capacity decreased by 50% compared with 2014. As a result, demand grew by 14.8% in 2017, while domestic natural gas production grew by only 8.2%.

Slow pipeline network construction and insufficient interconnection have restricted the allocation of resources and the guarantee of market supply. In 2014-2016, demand growth for natural gas slowed. With lower returns on investment in the new pipeline network and cutbacks in construction funding, the average annual increase in mileage was only 5,000 km. By the end of 2017, China's natural gas pipeline mileage was about 74,000 km. For every 10,000 km^2 of land, the pipeline mileage was about 77 km, which was only 15% of that of the United States. The pipeline network's load (319 cubic metres per kilometre of natural gas consumption per mile) was twice that of the United States. There was a low degree of interconnection among the main pipelines, among the main pipelines and the provincial pipeline network, and among the coastal LNG receiving stations and the main pipelines. Regional gas source "isolated island" or LNG isolated stations existed in many places. There were few hub stations with an interconnection function and fewer pipelines with a two-way gas transmission function. The pipe network pressure did not match, and the surplus gas source and the capacity of the LNG receiving station could not be utilized effectively. By the end of 2017, the natural gas pipeline network was interconnected in three places among the three major oil companies,[4] resulting in considerable constraints on the allocation of resources and the maintenance of supply in the market. In addition, the refined reform program for the separation of pipeline network transport and sales has not yet been introduced. Although gas supply enterprises carried out, in the enterprise level, related

[4] At the end of 2017, the natural gas pipeline network was interconnected in three places. The West-East gas transmission line 2 and the Sichuan-east gas transmission pipeline were interconnected at the Hubei Wuxue gas compressor station, the West-East gas transmission line 2 and Guangdong pipeline network at the Guangzhou gas compressor station, and Shaanxi-Beijing line and Anping-Ji'nan gas transmission line at the Anping gas compressor station.

to measures on the separation of natural gas transport and sales business, there was still a great gap from the spirit of the reform documents. Some provincial pipeline network enterprises also retained the "unified purchase and marketing" mode of operation, restricting the formation of regional market-oriented competition.

Due to the rapid growth of imported gas, and the lack of resource balance and security, the diversified supply system needs to be improved. China's dependence on foreign natural gas has risen rapidly, with imported gas volume rising rapidly from 17.5 billion cubic meters in 2010 to 94.6 billion cubic meters in 2017. Although the sources of imports have exceeded 20 countries and regions, the volume of gas imports is mainly concentrated in Turkmenistan, Australia, and Qatar. Supply from the three countries accounts for more than 70% of China's imports. Uncertainty over natural gas import guarantees has increased. Turkmenistan, Uzbekistan, Kazakhstan and China are geographical of the same latitude. In winter, the imported pipeline gas is easily affected by cold waves, resulting in short-term supply shortages. The LNG import is affected by such factors as the weather, sea conditions and navigation channels, and the uncontrollable factors have increased. Therefore, it is urgent to establish a natural gas import resource guarantee mechanism.

If liability is not clearly defined, there is no sufficient restraint. The imperfect auxiliary service market mechanism has led to the serious shortage of gas storage capacity. In 2014, the National Development and Reform Commission issued the Order No. 8. Local governments were required to have three days of gas storage capacity, and gas supply enterprises were required to have 10% gas storage capacity. However, there were shortcomings in the implementation of the policy. Based on underground gas storage depots and LNG receiving stations, and supplemented by gas energy conservation on land as well as large-scale CNG and LNG storage, there is still a long way to go for the construction of the gas storage system supported by the interconnection of pipeline networks. In the meantime, there is insufficient supervision and implementation for the capacity building of gas storage peak shaving. The completion of upstream gas storage indicators is lagging behind, and downstream users are over-dependent on upstream peak shaving for a long period of time. Due to the imperfect gas storage peak shaving market mechanism, the market value of gas storage facilities lacks price realization methods, and the construction operation investment cost lacks recovery channels. In addition, the auxiliary service market has not been established, and the enterprises have low investment enthusiasm. As of the end of 2017, underground gas storage has formed an effective working gas volume of 7.7 billion cubic meters, accounting for 3.2% of China's apparent consumption, far below the world average of 12%~15%. The storage capacity of the 18 LNG receiving stations reaches 4 billion cubic meters. The total gas storage capacity is seriously insufficient. It is difficult to play roles demanding the adjusting seasonal demand fluctuations, coping with supply risks and stabilizing market prices.

(2) Insufficient policy coordination and support strength have led to phased imbalances in the development of the natural gas industry.

First, inter-departmental, inter-industry coordination is not smooth, and the coordinated development system of the entire industrial chain has not yet formed. Forced by the impact of the evaluation, all regions have currently introduced various environmental protection policies and focused on environmental protection supervision. The project of "changing coal into gas" was suddenly rectified, reformed, and promoted in a concentrated manner. Much of the work from 2013 to 2017 was carried out in 2017, making it difficult to predict the market balance. It should be noted that in addition to the residential demand for "changing coal into gas", the industrial demand for "changing coal into gas" increased more considerably. Neither the supply nor the infrastructure of the current natural gas industry can support the surge in demand in the short term. In the meantime, at present, environmental protection policies on the consumption side require the rapid expansion of natural gas consumption, while those on the supply side have formed a hard constraint on increasing production and supply of natural gas. According to preliminary estimates, the current production capacity for producing and processing natural gas to be withdrawn according to environmental and ecological protection requirements is equivalent to 10 million tons of production capacity.

Second, the price reform has not yet been fully implemented. The pricing mechanism of provincial gate station price linked to alternative energy has not been dynamically adjusted. The peak-valley gas price mechanism has not been fully formed. The economic means to encourage users to participate in peak shaving is not sufficient. It is difficult to give full play to the role of the price in balancing supply and demand. The phenomena of gas price cross-subsidy and gas price dropping away from the state purchasing prices still exist, which affect the residential gas supply in winter. With a low degree of participation in market transactions, natural gas trading centres have fewer participants in online transactions, and the ways and means of transactions are relatively single. A market-based natural gas trading system in line with China's national conditions needs to be further explored and formed.

Third, it is increasingly difficult to select pipelines for such linear engineering systems as pipelines and to coordinate the construction of the projects. Some infrastructure projects are difficult to implement due to such policy restrictions as land use, sea area use and protected areas. The tax sharing system has not been implemented in the construction and operation of pipelines. Even regions with less income must bear the responsibility of pipeline safety protection. Therefore, local enthusiasm is generally not high. Under the combined influences, the pipeline construction and operation, oil and gas pipeline and road coordination are becoming increasingly difficult. Land acquisition is obstructed, examination and approval are not smooth. As a result, project advancement has been restricted.

Fourth, the natural gas supply guarantee mechanism and the emergency disposal mechanism are imperfect. Due to the lack of unified standards and supervision, in the case of the two-track price system, some responsible parties, for economic interests, cannot guarantee people's priority to use gas. The interconnection coordination mechanism and business model need to be improved. No long-term coordination mechanism has been established for daily operation and emergency status. Business cooperation mode is still the mode of "one issue, one discussion". There is no procedural, standardized, market-oriented cooperation mode.

Fifth, the fiscal and tax support policies for the development of natural gas need to be further matched. The exploration and development of tight sandstone gas reserves on a considerable scale need to be supported by policies. The economic benefit of shale gas and coalbed methane development is still low. The R&D support for key theories, technology and core equipment is limited. The core technology of exploration and development of deep and volcanic gas reservoirs are lacking. The key technology and equipment for deepwater oil and gas development are still mainly imported. There is still a great gap between the engineering technology of shale gas and coalbed methane development and the world advanced level. The core technology of deep shale gas and continental shale gas development are still awaiting breakthroughs. The R&D of key technology and the localization of advanced equipment in natural gas exploration, development and utilization are in urgent need of greater policy support.

3. Accelerate the Construction of Natural Gas Production, Supply, Storage and Marketing System, Support the Coordinated and Stable Development of the Industry

Natural gas is a high-quality, high-efficiency, green and clean low-carbon energy. Accelerating the development and utilisation of natural gas and promoting its stable coordinated development is an important path for China to steadily boost its energy production and consumption revolution and to establish a clean, safe, low-carbon, and high-efficiency energy system. Accelerating the development and utilization of natural gas is an organic part of the people's yearning for a beautiful life, and is an inevitable requirement in the Blue Sky Protection Campaign and Pollution Prevention and Control Campaign. With the explosive growth of domestic consumption in 2017, the main energy status of natural gas has been further established. However, during the heating season in 2017—2018, the tension supply in some local areas showed some prominent problems. For example, the current production, supply and marketing system is not sound, and the reform of the industrial chain system and mechanism is out of step. In the crucial period of securing a decisive victory in building a moderately prosperous society in all respects, we must be guided by Xi Jinping's Thought of Socialism with Chinese Characteristics for a New Era to implement the decisions and arrangements of the CPC Central Committee and the State Council on deepening the reform of the oil and natural gas system, and the tasks and requirements of speeding up the construction of the natural gas production, supply, storage, and marketing system to solve the problem of the unbalanced and uncoordinated development of natural gas. This will ensure that supply and demand of natural gas will be basically balanced, the population's gas consumption will be effectively guaranteed, market rules will be fully respected, and that the natural gas industry will develop healthily, orderly, and sustainably.

(1) Rapid development period under the background of the New Era in the natural gas industry in China

The Chinese government attaches great importance to the coordinated and stable development of natural gas. The National Development and Reform Commission and National Energy Administration together with the Ministry of Natural

Resources, Ministry of Ecological Environment, Ministry of Finance, Ministry of Housing and Urban-Rural Development and Ministry of Transport strive to regard the construction of the natural gas production, supply, storage, and marketing system as a key task; all departments, places and enterprises shall center on the people, and regard ensuring the stable supply of natural gas as an important livelihood project and political project with positive planning and sound promotion. All departments shall, through the inter-ministerial joint meeting mechanism and weekly meeting mechanism, promote the promulgation of relevant support policies, such as finance and taxation policy and project approval, conduct effective coordination and take forceful measures to promote the rapid implementation of the supply guarantee project.

The consensus of vigorous development in natural gas is gradually being formed throughout the whole society. First, after years of development, it has become common knowledge that natural gas is low-carbon, highly efficient and safe and reliable. Its position as a clean energy source enjoys popular support. The report of the 19th National Congress of the Communist Party of China indicated that the principal social contradiction of China has transformed into a contradiction between the people's increasing demands for a better life and unbalanced and inadequate development. The development of natural gas is related to the national economy and the people's livelihood, and clean heating reflects people's yearning for green water and mountains. Accelerating the development and utilization of natural gas has become an important part of China's transformation of energy development. The high attention of governments at all levels has aroused the deep focus of the society and media, who are optimistic about the future development trend of the natural gas industry. Second, under the guidance of system reform, forced appraisal, and policy support, the vitality of each link of the industry chain is gradually released to support the rapid development of natural gas in China.

The international market environment supports the rapid development of natural gas in China. The relatively loose international LNG market environment is facilitative of the rapid development of natural gas in China. The rapid development of the international LNG market greatly breaks through the limitation of traditional pipeline transportation and boosts the efficient circulation of natural gas among various markets around the world. As of the end of 2017, 34 LNG projects have been put into production around the world. There are 102 production lines, with a total production capacity of

355 million tons/year. It is estimated that there will be 15 LNG projects under construction in 2020, mainly distributed in Africa, North America, Europe and the Asia-Pacific region with a total planned production capacity of about 92.7 million tons. As LNG projects under construction in Australia, Russia and the United States are gradually put into production, it is expected that the world's new LNG supply will exceed 100 million tons/year by 2020. Demands of traditional Asian LNG import countries, such as China (including Taiwan), South Korea, and India, as well as Europe are expected to be huge in the next few years, while demands of emerging markets, such as, Pakistan, the Philippines and Bangladesh are expected to grow faster. In general, by 2020, the overall supply in the international LNG market is relatively loose, but it will still be characterized by seasonal supply tension in individual areas.

(2) The construction of coordinated and stable production, supply, storage and marketing system for natural gas in China

The construction of a coordinated and stable production, supply, storage and marketing system for natural gas mainly includes accelerating domestic exploration and development, improve overseas multivariate supply, establish a multi-level natural gas reserve system, accelerate the construction of natural gas infrastructure and pipeline network interconnection, accurately predict market demand and establish an early warning mechanism, establish a sound graded contingency plan for natural gas supply, establish and perfect natural gas demand side management and peak shaving mechanism, establish a comprehensive coordinating mechanism for natural gas development, rationalize the price of natural gas and accelerate the pace of structural reform, etc. The construction of natural gas production, supply, storage and marketing system cannot be accomplished in a single action with lasting efficiency. It is a systematic engineering project, and the function of mechanism operation is also progressive, so it requires the concerted cooperation of the locality, the departments and the oil and gas enterprises.

Firstly, accelerate the formation of an orderly and competitive market mechanism for exploration and development. We will strictly implement block withdrawal and comprehensively implement the competitive transfer of blocks. We will vigorously promote the joint venture between the central and the local entity and leave taxes for the locality to achieve mutual benefit and mutual development. We will accelerate the research and formulation of the competitive transfer mechanism of difficult-to-produce and marginal reserves, and vitalize the stock of reserves by adopting multiple measures. We will strengthen the support capability assessment of state-owned oil and gas enterprises. The enterprises shall serve for national energy strategies. We will appropriately reduce economic indicator constraints for exploration and development activities and effectively increase the effective supply. For example, it is expected that the implementation of unconventional natural gas investment projects, such as tight gas, shale gas and coalbed methane shall be promoted based on the internal rate of return of 6%. Meanwhile, the special action plan for an increase in reserves and production has been formed in main production areas in Sichuan Basin, Erdos and Xinjiang. We will coordinate the relationship between natural gas development and environmental protection to avoid the dilemma that “the consumption side requires expanding natural gas consumption while the exploration and development activities of the supply side are limited everywhere”.

Secondly, improve diversification of overseas supply system for natural gas. We will constantly optimize the import structure and layout of natural gas in China both in the sea and on land, accelerate the diversification of regions, transportation modes, import channels and contract modes of natural gas import countries, and actively and orderly promote the diversification of import entities. We will ensure the import and attach equal importance to import trade and overseas investment. In terms of import trade, long-term and spot goods shall be controlled. While increasing the stable supply of natural gas, we will give full play to the market-oriented peak regulation of spot resources. In terms of overseas investments, we will highlight benefit development, support the enterprises to invest in the upstream exploration and development of overseas natural gas, and enhance the control ability of imported natural gas resources. We will strengthen bilateral cooperation with key natural gas exporting countries, make clear key projects of international cooperation and accelerate the implementation.

Thirdly, strengthen the construction of gas storage capacity and establish a multi-level reserve system. The multi-level gas storage peak-shaving system will be built with the underground gas storage depots and coastal LNG receiving stations as the focus, inland incentivization of key regions and emergency large-scale LNG storage as the auxiliary, and the interconnection of pipeline network as the support. The gas storage capacity of gas supply enterprises shall be no less than 10% of their annual contracted sales capacity by 2020. By 2020, the gas storage capacity of urban gas enterprises shall be no less than 5% of their annual gas consumption. Meanwhile, the *Regulations on the Administration of Urban Gas* and the *Design Standards of Urban Gas* will be revised accordingly. By 2020, the local government shall form a gas storage capacity that is no less than the average daily consumption of 3 days in the administrative region. As a temporary transitional measure, if the gas storage capacity fails to meet the requirements, the peak shaving capacity shall be implemented by signing the interruptible gas supply contract. The provincial people's governments shall be responsible for coordinating and promoting the gas storage capacity of local governments and urban gas enterprises and the intensive, large-scale operation of gas storage facilities to avoid "flourishing everywhere". We will strengthen the tracking and dispatching of the construction of gas storage capacity, and conduct respond-on-demand accountability and associated disciplinary punishment on the behaviors, such as, ineffective promotion, violations and breaching promises, etc.

Forthly, improve the construction of natural gas infrastructure and interconnection promotion mechanism. We will accelerate the construction of the planned pipeline and LNG receiving station, etc., and promote the interconnection of pipelines. We will strengthen the plans for all levels of infrastructure construction, and the cohesion among infrastructure construction plan, plans for land space, urban and rural construction, land and sea use and forest land occupation, and ecological protection red lines, especially the requirements for land and sea use shall be ensured for the project. We will implement the spirit of simpler administration and empowerment, simplify and optimize the examination and approval of the prepositive documents, actively implement parallel approval and post-approval changed from pre-approval, and shorten the compliance construction procedures and approval cycle of the project. The implementation plan of the LNG storage and transportation system of Bohai Rim Region shall be formulated as soon as possible in the short-medium term to ensure the safe supply of natural gas in Beijing-Tianjin and Hebei regions and the surrounding areas and Fenwei Plain. Intensive layout and scale development of LNG receiving stations encourages multi-entities construction, and encourage sharing of station sites and seashore resources; priority shall be given to extension and new construction of the harbour area near the existing LNG receiving stations with favourable conditions and relatively mature preliminary work. We will strengthen the overall plan of the stations to form an external transmission pipeline covering the main consumption area of the coastal area, interconnecting with national trunk pipeline network and further radiating to the inland. We will accelerate and improve the national trunk pipe network in medium and long term to a form network system with main consumption areas and production areas of natural gas in the whole country, two-way transportation of key nodes and key lines, and fully connected imported and domestic gas, multi-gas source, cross-regional and inter-regional peak shaving and cooperative protection. We will conduct special supervision over the natural gas infrastructure and interconnection major projects.

Fifthly, establish an integrated coordination mechanism for natural gas development. We will strengthen the contractual spirit of both parties to promote the signing of the comprehensive contract by gas enterprises and encourage the signing of the medium and long term contract. "Changing coal into gas" shall adhere to "gas-oriented changing", and shall be designedly promoted under the premise of implementing the air supply; key areas, such as Beijing-Tianjin-Hebei regions and surrounding areas shall be highlighted, and the orderly and simultaneous advancement shall be guaranteed. We will establish and perfect a credit system in the field of natural gas, and conduct joint punishment to regions and enterprises breaching the contract and failing to ensure the supply in the dishonest list for their severe behaviours of violating of laws and breaching of promises according to the circumstances. The financial subsidy policy of shale gas and coalbed methane will be extended to the "14th Five-year Plan" period, and the volume of exploitation and utilization of tight gas is supported by financial subsidies. We will research to provide central financial subsidies for purchasing expenditure of bottom gas in underground gas storage construction, and provide financial subsidies within the central budgets for the construction of emergency gas storage facilities in key areas Based on the evaluation and argumentation of third-party organizations, we will study the policy of VAT return in import link of LNG receiving station projects according to the actual loading and unloading volume. We will actively develop transportation with small LNG ships off the coast and inland rivers, and promote the promulgation of relevant laws, regulations, standards and specifications and standards on LNG cylinder multimodal transport.

Sixthly, establish and perfect the demand side management of natural gas, refine the early warning, peak shaving and emergency mechanisms. We will consider various factors, such as economic development, urbanization process, energy structure adjustment and price policy, etc., to accurately predict natural gas demand, especially sub-structure demand in winter heating period. We will establish an early-warning mechanism for natural gas supply and demand, timely predict and warn the emerging, tendentious and potential problems of supply and demand, and perfect the communication and feedback mechanism to ensure the connection between supply and demand. We will stick to the rational and efficient utilization of natural gas. The amount of newly added natural gas is preferred for the life of urban residents and areas with serious air pollution and the replacement of bunk coal in winter heating. We will focus on supporting the Beijing-Tianjin-Hebei regions and surrounding areas and Fenwei Plain to realize the "gas-increasing and coal-reducing". We will research to introduce the regulations on peak shaving users, establish and perfect the system of graded peak shaving users, and start the implementation in time according to the principle of "ensuring safety, advance notification, adequate communication and proper advancement". The local people's governments at all levels shall bear the responsibility of the main entities for ensuring the supply of the livelihood gas, and the people's governments at or above the county level, the upstream gas supply enterprises and the urban gas enterprises shall, according to the principle of "controlling the non-resident gas and ensuring the resident gas", prepare the graded ensuring plan and the user peak shaving plan. We will establish a reasonable cost allocation mechanism for ensuring the supply of natural gas. Relevant responsibilities of corresponding emergency expenditure shall be fully undertaken by the party who fails to ensure the supply, and the third party enterprise participating in ensuring the supply may obtain reasonable benefits.

Seventhly, straighten out the price mechanism of natural gas. We will implement the parallel price policy for resident and non-resident gate stations, and reasonably guide the sale price of gas for household use. We will encourage the urban gas enterprises to establish the upstream and downstream gas price linkage mechanism, and encourage the regions with favourable conditions to first release the sale price of large customer terminals. We will encourage and support the gas supply enterprises and natural gas users to negotiate and establish a peak shaving price mechanism. We will reduce the air supply level, strengthen the regulation of gas distribution links, and earnestly reduce the extortionate pipeline transportation price and gas distribution price in the province. We will encourage users to independently choose resources and air supply path and form, vigorously develop the dual gas supply and multi-gas supply for the region and users. We will implement local main responsibility and give subsidies to the low-income group, families conducting "changing coal into gas" in the northern rural areas to ensure that the living standard of the low-income group will not be reduced by price reform. We must strengthen the supervision and inspection of natural gas price, and investigate and punish price violations. The Central Finance shall make full use of funds for air pollution prevention to increase supports and guarantee the smooth implementation of reform policies. We will orderly promote the construction of spot market of natural gas, and build a unified and open natural gas market system with orderly competition, consisting of futures trading platforms and several regional spot trading platforms and covering the main consumption areas of natural gas, such as, Bohai Sea, South China, Central China and Sichuan-Chongqing regions. By learning from the successful experience of crude oil futures and relying on the construction of LNG storage and transportation system around the Bohai Sea, the natural gas futures are released for trial.

Eighthly, accelerate the structural reform of natural gas. *Opinions on Deepening the Reform of the Oil and Gas System* promulgated by the Central Committee of CPC is implemented to promote the implementation and effectiveness of reforms. We will deepen oil and gas exploration and mining management, earnestly strengthen domestic resources exploration and development efforts, introduce structural reform program of natural gas pipeline network as soon as possible, define market expectancy and encourage enterprises to invest in the construction of pipeline network. We will urge enterprises to provide the infrastructure including natural gas pipeline network fairly and openly for the third-party market entities. We will accelerate the release of the right to use the geological structure of gas storage, and perfect the leasing, transferring, abandonment and write-off mechanism of the mining rights in oil and gas and salt industry and the evaluation mechanism of developed oil & gas fields and salt mines. We will encourage oil and gas enterprises and salt enterprises to cooperate with other entities to construct underground gas storage by making use of exhausted oil and gas reservoirs and salt cavities (including old cavities and newly-built ones).

Concluding Remarks

In the context of tackling climate change and promoting green and low-carbon energy transformation worldwide, natural gas ushered in a rare historical opportunity for development by following the new two-step strategy proposed at the 19th National Congress of the Communist Party of China to vigorously promote the construction of an ecological civilization, to fight decisively and triumphantly the battle in defense of the blue skies, and to build beautiful China.

The year 2018 will continue to be a year of rapid natural gas growth, with apparent consumption expected to be around 271 billion cubic meters (excluding supplies to Hong Kong and Macao), an increase of 13.5% year-on-year. However, the growth rate will undergo a slowdown from 2017. Among them, industrial fuel gas consumption will increase significantly with an estimated 90 billion cubic meters, accounting for 33.2%. The year-on-year growth rate will be 18.4%. Urban gas and natural gas power generation are expected to maintain a rapid growth with consumption estimated to be 105 billion cubic meters and 50 billion cubic meters, accounting for 38.7% and 18.5%, respectively. Chemical engineering gas consumption will continue to be sluggish, at about 26 billion cubic meters, accounting for less than 10%. It is estimated that the proportion of natural gas in the primary energy consumption structure will increase to nearly 10%, 14% and 15% respectively in 2020, 2030 and 2050.

For the natural gas industry in China, 2018 is not only a year full of challenges but a year of deepening reform and time spent building a system for natural gas production, supply, storage and marketing. China must maintain the bottom line—the safety of China's natural gas development, ensure the safe and stable supply of natural gas and meet the people's increasing demand for gas. In the meantime, we should be aware that we will face the short term challenges of strengthening the construction of infrastructure such as peak shaving, accelerating the increase in reserves and production, and building a diversified supply system. These many difficulties must be overcome, and the work must be completed in an efficient and high-quality manner with the energy of driving home a nail.

By 2018, the White Paper on *China Natural Gas Development Report* has been successfully launched for the last three years, setting up a communication platform for promoting China's energy transformation and exploring the healthy and rapid development of the natural gas industry. It is expected that the release of the *China Natural Gas Development Report (2018)* will further stimulate consensus among all sectors of society to jointly promote the construction of natural gas production, supply, storage, and marketing system. Here, we sincerely extend our thanks to the relevant departments, research institutions, industry associations, enterprises, international institutions and many experts for their help and support.